SYNERGY
POETRY & MUSINGS

WENDY C. GARFINKLE

SYNERGY

POETRY & MUSINGS

WENDY C. GARFINKLE

Emery Press, LLC
Fort Lauderdale, FL
www.emerypressbooks.com

All rights reserved

First Edition – April 2022
Copyright 2022 – Wendy C Garfinkle
https://www.wendycgarfinkle.com/

No part of this book may be reproduced or transmitted in any form or by any means, electronic or mechanical, including photocopying, recording, or by any information storage and retrieval system, except as permitted by law. For additional information contact Emery Press Books.

ISBN (Trade): 978-1-7364295-5-6
ISBN (eBook): 978-1-7364295-6-3

Cover Design by Sweet 15 Designs
Editing by Grammar Goddess Editing

For you who understand

TABLE OF CONTENTS

BODY 11
    A Singer's Voice 13
    Adrenaline Rush 15
    Growing Pains 17
    I am woman 19
    iPod 21
    Migraine 23
    More than just a piece of "tail" 25
    Ode to a Dear Friend Who Lives in a Bottle 27
    pretty little girl 29
    She: Pronoun 31
    Sunrise in Flight 33
    Surviving 35
    the dance (part 1) 37
    This Body: Motherhood 39
    Would I Be Accepted? 43

HEART 47
    Actions Speak Louder than Words 49
    Certainty; Illusion 51
    Collaboration 53
    compromising with my son 55
    Crystal Ball 57
    embrace the pain 59

game of hearts 61

Heart Sister (For Scarlett) 63

If 65

Impatience and Equanimity 67

In Ink 69

love. (lost?) 71

let me heal you 75

magnet poetry 79

Sensation 81

You: A fantasy 83

MIND 85

Anticipation 87

Battle 89

Blood is red; veins are blue 91

Coin Toss 93

Crash and Burn 97

Depression (From the Inside Out) 99

~~effervescent~~ me 111

Freedom (in America) 113

Images of Wilkes-Barre 115

~~Innocence~~ 117

Inspiration 119

Journey 121

Loose Lips Sink Ships 123

My Future 125

neglect	127
Off the grid	129
Overcast	131
Panic Attack	133
Rainstorm during a traffic jam	137
red light	139
Silence	141
Stronger Than You Think	143
The Summer of His Discontent	145
Weather Witch (Dennah)	147
SOUL	**149**
A Lifetime Supply	151
A Prayer for the Dying	153
A Still Small Voice: Elijah's Song	155
Are you happier now?	161
As you were	163
Candle-less	167
Does God Make Mistakes?	169
Forget Me Not	173
Formed in the Fire	175
Grace (or, The Golden Trumpet Tree)	177
He Came	179
Hope Renewed	183
Not My Will	185
Our Weakness; His Strength	187

Recovery 189

Splinter.. 193

Stumble or Rise... 195

Surrender 197

That Sounds Like Home to Me 199

What does God do? 201

Which Path? 203

Publishing Acknowledgements **205**

About the Author.. **207**

BODY

Merriam-Webster: *"the main, central, or principal part; the organized physical substance...such as the material part or nature of a human being"*

"For you formed my inward parts; you knitted me together in my mother's womb. I praise you, for I am fearfully and wonderfully made." **(Psalm 139:13-14, ESV)**

A Singer's Voice

a singer's voice
rusty from years of disuse –

(*your gifts*
don't always
make a way for you.
Sometimes they
lay
                    forgotten
in the
dust)

– wavers
as she struggles
to hit the key.

worship songs,
half an hour twice a week
aren't enough
        practice
for a once-vibrant
voice.

she sighs and wonders

SYNERGY

if
her tones
will ever – again
rise
    strong and true.

Adrenaline Rush

Cradle the headset in my sweaty palm
   fingers poised to dial the number
anything but calm
   don't stop to analyze and wonder
                      just
                      dial.

Hear the huskiness in your voice
   when you answer my call
the breathlessness at the end;
   enchanted and enthralled.

Quickly in a heady rush
   I state my business
no need to push;
   the next step...yours.

Returned to normal
   back to earth...
yet not all is calm
   palms sweat, hands shake...
      Adrenaline rush.

Growing Pains

In ancient times
my pen knew how to write
   imagination soared
   images freely flowed into words.
Time travel was possible
   so many dreams came true
   through the flow of my pen.

Now
when the fantastic
   begs to take form
my pen betrays me.
I find no more solace on paper.
   dreams cannot take shape
the words to tell of them are lost to me.
All my wanderings locked deep within my soul.

Nightmares greet dreams as they journey
through the tunnels of my imagination.
Desires bid farewell to convictions
   as one by one
they depart for more fertile ground.

SYNERGY

Tears comforted by laughter
as they await the pleasure of my emotions.

I am woman

i am

                woman

i am

                female

in all of my incarnations

i am

      both

noun and adjective

i am

      myself

and i describe myself

                as

female human being

iPod

my questing fingers search
for the slick metal of my new "woobie"
>   *(a term left over from my marriage to a man*
>   *who is fond of such made-up terms)*
the tiny iridescent purple square
already feeling familiar in my grasp.

Migraine

random
    thoughts
    images
stomp
the inside of my skull
with
       size-13 steel-toe booted feet

p r e s s u r i n g

my head to vibrate and spasm
      under the direction of a
sadistic maestro
as veins pulse, pound
      to their rhythm,
bloated with blood, wrenched out of shape.

head in a vise
brain on fire
mirages in my vision

    tiny
        red
            ball

SYNERGY

                                  bounces

a blur before my eyes

stomach churns
bile fills my mouth
a whimper escapes my lips
close my eyes for a moment of relief
halos strobe behind my lids
open them again

migraine awaits

More than just a piece of "tail"

Why
are men so fixated on what's

                 beneath

a woman's clothing?

What about what's beneath her skin

            (*not as in dissection or autopsy*)

or between her ears?

What about how she
     walks
     talks
     thinks?

What about
her relationships with
     her mother
     her father
     her siblings?
Or what kind of mother she is
     (*if she is one*)?

SYNERGY

I know of sexting.

I've been there before
      ... years since.
I felt dirty

          (not in a good way)

cheap
used
unloved
unsatisfied
And that was with someone
with whom I shared mutual respect,
love and years-long friendship.

I like to take the measure of a man.
      (Who he is as a person
      is more important
      than the pleasure his limbs and digits
      can give my body.)

Not every man can endure that scrutiny.

Ode to a Dear Friend Who Lives in a Bottle

You became my best friend
Though I didn't know you for long
A mutual acquaintance introduced us,
    thought we'd work well together.
You comforted me through my illness
    made it more endurable.
I spent as much time with you as I could
    while careful to avoid accusations of "forgetting old friends."

And then one day without warning you were

GONE!

I was bewildered and hurt;
    was it something I had done,
    something that I said?

I went to all your old haunts
You weren't there;
    left no forwarding address.
Asked those I thought would know where to find you;
    they didn't.

SYNERGY

I was desperate; the illness
      was unbearable without you
So I turned to other assistance

anything to stop the pain;
but it wasn't the same.
For months, I felt lost without you
      Nowhere I looked, could I find you

Then yesterday, I revisited one of your old spots
and looked for you, on a whim.

There you were!

Your beloved features beaming at me.
I laughed, cried, greeted you with a grin

At last! We're together again
My dear, beloved,
    Excedrin Migraine!

pretty little girl

TRIGGER WARNING: *Child Sex Abuse*

pretty little girl
blonde pixie of a child
big green eyes
barely 4 years from birth.

"do you want some candy?"

of course she does.

he tells her to be quiet
so they don't wake her baby brother
sleeping nearby in his crib.

they slip from the room
in stocking feet.
in the kitchen
he feeds her chocolate.

innocent child plays a game

"bet you don't know i'm not wearing any panties."

SYNERGY

*(the grown woman that child became
shakes her head violently in warning
but knows there's no saving the little girl
who loved to play games with her friends.)*

at his mocking disbelief and challenge of
"show me"
the child pulls away her p.j.s, and shows off
her naked, tiny vagina.

did the idea enter his head then
to invade her body,
believing that when a 4-year-old says "yes"
she's
      old enough,
      wise enough,
to consent?

or was the intent there already
and the innocent child
played into his design?

She: Pronoun

She

        anonymous
        non-descriptive

Pronoun.

Does
She
Have a name?

Or is
She
    Identity-less
A mere
    extension
Of you?

Sunrise in Flight
(Over Britain, Summer 1998)

an ocean of clouds
stretching as far as my eye can see
silent and still
silver lining secreted in their billowy depths.

the sun
making its majestic way above the horizon
deep night giving way
to the fire of a brand new dawn.

and the world is
reborn.

Surviving

TRIGGER WARNING: *Attempted Rape*

If I could paint a picture . . .

The colors would all be shades of violence, rage and depression
> stark, bloody reds
> midnight blues
> black streaks
> bruised purples
> sickly greens

back-grounding

The tense lines of her body
> Blonde hair a halo
around her furious, bleak face
> icy blue eyes
> glaring
Down
  at him
Her slight weight
> Pinning him to her bed

SYNERGY

The bed he invaded,
        unwelcomed

His arms restrained
held in place by her rigid, muscular limbs
as she straddles his trunk

Her angry palm flat against his chest
Burning
       her hatred
              into his bare flesh

while she holds, with her other hand

              Her Beretta M9
pressed firmly
      against his skull.

the dance (part 1)

dance with me
feel the rhythm and be
step to the strains
rising through our feet

dance with me
take my hand
with your imagination see
the savage beauty

dance with me
raw desire
sparks with our motion
fan the fire

dance with me
feel the music and be
take my hand
and share the mystery.

This Body: Motherhood

I do not recognize this body. . .
    Oh, the changes that motherhood brings!
that created
    conceived in the usual manner...
grew
    and as he grew, so did I...
        into roughly the size of a beached whale...
shielded
    tiny feet River-Dancing on my bladder at all hours...
a tiny human
    for this child I prayed
        a son, and God gave
for nine point five months

    a defect in the heart
            mine
    demanded early ejection...

until he was
sucked – unwillingly
    extracted via vacuum, if you really must know...
from the matrix

I don't recognize this body. . .

SYNERGY

and morn
the trim, flat belly I never understood how to love
until it was forever gone

its elasticity stretched and strained beyond repair
the slim hips and thighs now
streaked
with wavy silver lines
    battle scars
the tangerine breasts that grew
into heavy grapefruit
    yet failed
to produce adequate colostrum and nourishment
for the tiny human boy

I don't recognize this body...
that never used to struggle with its own weight
metabolism ever churning to keep it trim and svelte
but now refuses to keep off the sturdy frame
those extra eighty or so pounds it was never meant to carry
the energy this body once harnessed, fled
with the birth of that small human boy
    I blame the method of extraction

I don't recognize this body...
once hated, ignored, disdained.
but revelation came,

when I remembered the traumas this body has endured
the battles fought and won
    growing & birthing a little human, among them

though never again to be what I once was,
better today than I was then

and this body...

this body is unique...
there will never be another of this model...

this body is to be loved and cherished
for as long as it breathes.

Would I Be Accepted?
(lessons from the left side of the fence)

Were I to be
   f l a y e d
of my ecru-hued skin and
   re-covered
with
      olive,
      mocha,
         or
      darker brown tone

   – (*it is a funny thing, whatever
      our skin tone,*
   WE. ALL. BLEED. RED.) –

would I
   THEN
be accepted
by you?

Were I to be
   h a r v e s t e d

of my
> "white"
>> heart

and
> ***transplanted***

with that of a descendant of a former slave
> **THEN**

would my heart
be accepted
by you?

Were I to choose my gender to be
> *f l u i d*

>> *(because make no mistake, it **IS** a choice)*

rather than

> **– AS GOD MADE ME –**

would I
> **THEN**

be
more acceptable

to you?

Were I to
    ignore
all the lessons I've absorbed,
all the research I've conducted,
all the prayers I have prayed,
all the life stories I've heard
        that have led me to
                think for myself
                      make up my own mind about what is right
                          and true
        instead of blindly following every wind that blows
in my 46 years

and swear by
        whatever you *feel*, is right
        abortion, for *any* reason
        globalism, *not* patriotism
        leaders are right *only* if you agree with them
        every woman is *always* right
                (*does that, then, make me something*
                        other *than a woman?*)

would I

SYNERGY

THEN

be acceptable
to you?

Were I to
denounce
the God in Whom I trust
the country to which I pledge my allegiance

Were I to
deny
my very existence
   everything
I hold as sacred and true
and instead be in lock-step with you
would I

THEN

be acceptable

    to

        you?

HEART

Merriam-Webster: *"the emotional or moral nature as distinguished from the intellectual nature: such as one's innermost character, feelings, or inclinations"*

"Above all else, guard your heart, for everything you do flows from it." **(Proverbs 4:23, NIV)**

Actions Speak Louder than Words

Speak to me
not with your
      words
but by your
      actions

Whisper sweet nothings in my ears
tell me you love me, but
show me,
too

Hold my hand
gaze into my eyes
touch me
let me see your face

actions speak
louder than
words

Words are just lip service.

Show me you care
by putting
action to your

SYNERGY

promises

Or else
shut up and
stop lying to me

Certainty; Illusion

So certain of certainty

                                                                         (illusion)

shattered in a moment

Sweetly, perilously
siren sings
temptation beckons
lures with a heated glance

Dance is bittersweet
thirst sated

                                   yet

hunger remains

Obsession takes hold
mind loathe to release
promise of the dance
and sweet mystery

Collaboration

My art
different
than yours.

You
paint upon
Canvas
    colors of bright, metallic, barren hues.
I
paint upon
Paper
    words of fluctuating shapes, sizes, complexities.

Both of us telling
       stories
evoking
       reactions
each in our own way.

Maybe we should
collaborate.

I'll
put words to your
       Colors.

SYNERGY

You
can lay images to my
      Letters.

compromising with my son

instead

of telling you to
turn down
your shoot-'em-up game
      and its accompanying cacophony
so I can
hear
the meandering classical instrumentations I've
chosen to listen to this rising,
I welcome them into the
          chaos
of my morning

Crystal Ball

Shining
    fine, murky, smoky
glass
fits
    smooth, cool
in my cupped hands.

Crystal ball,
show me what I most long to see
the face of he
who will be true to only me.
Show me my dear one
eyes
shining with love and passion
when he gazes at
me.

When will we be together?
Show me my future,
Crystal ball.
Bring him to me
now.

SYNERGY

And slipping from my
    grasping, desperate
fingers
Smooth, round

        p o w e r l e s s

glass falls through space
shattering silence
to lie in a million pieces at my feet.

embrace the pain

You walked
      willingly
    both
        eyes
           open
into your situation.

Feet planted
      firmly
on that path
knowing it may hurt you.

You cannot then cry
    foul
when the pain is
unexpectedly
    sharper
    deeper
than you anticipated.

You knew this could happen.

Embrace the pain
draw it to your bosom.

SYNERGY

    paradise
    mercy
may be the
eye of the hurricane
amidst the
despair.

game of hearts

too much trouble,
this
game of hearts

i
die a little
each time

stomach roils
bile boils
hot flashes,

        (not a menopausal symptom)

are you worth
this anxiety and derangement?

so much easier
so much calmer
        to dream and imagine
than
        to stretch out my hands
and
            fail

SYNERGY

to hold on to
                a happily ever after

reach
    too far
grasp
    too tight
want
    too much

no mystery to
an open book

game of hearts
grows bitter and sour
upon the tongue

Heart Sister (For Scarlett)

I was not blessed with
      a sister of my blood.

Instead a better blessing
      a sister of my heart
for we chose each other
and hold that much dearer.

She is to me
all that beauty should be
      in word and deed
her inner light shines bright
      illuminates every room.

Her
      worship and vocals
      loyalty to family and friends
      dedication to her profession
      love of people

   inspire and encourage me.

No envy or strife have I ever borne for her
as might for a sister in flesh
for though frailty and faults plague us both

SYNERGY

as with all who be of human flesh and bone
I cherish her love and friendship

given
    without reservation
    without condition
and returned in equal measure.

Though a generation of years divide us
    (myself, Gen X; her, Gen Y)
the connection and affection of kindred hearts
bridge the gap.

I wish
I demand
only the best that life can offer her

and
    pray
    trust
each day in the God we serve to
    protect her
    guide her
along the path He has made, just for her.

I love you always,
dearest Scarlett Olivia,
    sister of my heart.

If . . .

For years
I have
mourned
the innocence
of you.

I have wondered . . .

                      IF

when we were young
and the military rearranged you

                      IF

I had come with you
would the man
with whom I fell in love –
    your charm
    your laughter
    your innocence –
have remained,
    matured
rather than soured?

SYNERGY

OR

as I became
> your wife
> your lover

would I
also
have become
> your mother?

Impatience and Equanimity

A shroud of silence
    envelops me
        as I watch the scene, the images
            materialize
        beneath your knowing hand

The vibrant shades on your canvas
            haunt me.

I feel the sharp stroke of your sable brush
    as you connect the jagged edges
        of our banter.

Your graceful hand moves
    slowly, leisurely
        across my being.

Gaps
        linger
            in the pattern
    of us.

Impatient
    I speak sharply;
    annoyed by your
        equanimity.

SYNERGY

You smile gently;
    slow is good,
        you reply.

In Ink

Pen scratches across the page
words formed in blue ink

>*(NOT black ink;*
>*maybe green or purple,*
>*red or pink;*
>*but NEVER black ink.)*

the old-fashioned way.

Words spill
on the page
as I transcribe my thoughts.
    images
     snap-shots
scroll behind my eyelids

Only once in a while
can
    mere
        words
capture the meaning
within the pictures.

SYNERGY

Texting is
    Informal

Phone calls are
    inconvenient

Letters, though,
    are just right
    for making connections
across the miles
that come between us

Connections...

    wanting to feel
        somehow
    closer to you

love. (lost?)
(for S.R.)

i remember you.
when first we met
i, barely more than a child
you, already touched by war.

two different worlds
                converging.

you
overcame my shyness
with your admiration for
my writing skills.

we
talked and exchanged numbers.

though we lived in the same town,
rarely met face-to-face;
hours would pass on the telephone (*pre-cellphone days*).

i remember you;
you said
i
ruined

SYNERGY

you
for any other woman.

but you kept returning
to them.

and then
      you
           let
                me
                    go

                          too easily.

(why didn't you fight for me
why didn't you tell me
                    THEN
how you felt?)

i
lost
you
again
years later
when i returned.

she

had ruined you
for any other woman . . .
     even me.
but we talked again
more now;

and just when i thought
there was hope for
us,
     you
         abruptly
            left
               me
                  for
                     another.

let me heal you
(for L.H.)

let me heal you
dearest friend,
fellow composer of verse.

i want to fix you;
    (not that there's anything
    wrong with you,
    but you push
    my depression button.)

i want to heal you
of
the melancholy I see
in your eyes.
(two depressed persons
in this friendship
is two, too many.)

i want to heal
your unhappiness
your bittersweet smile

i want to find your
happily ever after

SYNERGY

for you

(*i want to BE*
your happily ever after)

but i fear –

     i know –

you will
never
let me
get that close to you

(*what do you fear?*)

let me
be
your *rephuah*
your muse
your love.

let me
heal
the hurt
that built a nest
inside of you

let me
wrap you
in the wings of
      my desire
      my love
      my respect
      my admiration

let me heal you

magnet poetry

his naked eyes
    embrace
    surround
me
in velvet poetry

lips
    warm
    on fire
melting my heart

voice dazzles me
lingering
                    magic
for eternity

he says
only you

Sensation

Images, part of my imagination
   pulp of a gutted fruit
lay silent and still
   lifeless – not breathing with the wind.

Stirred-up
   dart swiftly
     leaving me breathless with sadness
       and longing.

Traveling at the speed of a glance
   I look into your eyes
     pupils dark with promise
       irises light with purpose.

I sink slowly into myself again
   slow the throbbing of my heart
     imagination gives way to reality
       remembrance of who, what, I am.

So near to me
   yet so far away from ideal.

I dream
I dream.

SYNERGY

When I drop my eyes from yours
   I remember . . .

You: A fantasy

You
were
a fantasy
a figment of
imagination.

I was studied
my psyche probed
and the perfect man
for me
was born out of whole cloth
        full grown.

I was
                      cat-fished.

MIND

Merriam-Webster: *"the element or complex of elements in an individual that feels, perceives, thinks, wills, and especially reasons"*

*"For God has not given us a spirit of fear, but of power and of love and of a sound mind." **(II Timothy 1:7, NKJV)***

Anticipation

Two dozen and more
   restless youths
   bored by their long journey
await, fidgety,
   the next witty remark
   from their model comedian.

Expectant, while he dreams up
   some worthy limerick from the depths
   of his fertile imagination
aided by two friends on either side
   who willingly fill the short intermissions
   with ideas from their own repertoire.

Finally, like the percolating of a coffee maker
   his imagination releases dialogue
      to his lips
lining up in humorous, chaotic order
   to be delivered to a worthy audience
   waiting with keen anticipation.

Battle

I want to take up a sword
a warrior in battle
and face the pain.

Why can it not be a
tangible
something
that I can see
that I can fight?

Why must it take away my breath,
wound on the inside?

The façade I present to the world seems
    normal
a frown
a distant look

                they cannot see

    the battle raging within
    the battering my psyche sustains
    the bleeding of my heart
    the ripping to shreds of my aorta
        my lungs

SYNERGY

as I struggle to
      breathe, to
     stand
and face this
monster.

                Depression

Blood is red; veins are blue

TRIGGER WARNING: Metaphysical poem about cutting

Roses are red
Violets are blue

Blood is red
Veins are blue

Knife is silver
    cold
against my wrist.

Control is what I seek
    control
that eludes me.

The red
snakes down
the silver
rivulets drip-dropping
to *ping*
on the tile floor.

SYNERGY

Cold now
my hand

blessed

silence

roars
in my head.

I
    control
the blood that falls
from my arm
to the floor below.

Coin Toss

When I was a child
I
    railed at
    argued with
those who
disagreed
with me.

Everything
was personal.

I wailed in
    anger
    impotence
    inability
to make others see
and agree
with me.

When I grew up
I understood
it's not personal
these debates
one side against the other

SYNERGY

it's
    ignorance

    fear
    intolerance.

I do not need to justify
my opinions, my beliefs
only stand by them and witness

time
    and life
will educate,
    communicate
    illuminate

and others will
either
stumble and fall
or
step up and rise
    climb
the mountain of wisdom.

Vitriol
    solves nothing
    starts wars,

    death
    estrangement.

Let us,
    instead,

drink tea and debate
as adults
our opinions. An honest, open discourse

agree to disagree
    if we must
each,
    tolerant
    respecting
the other's right to be
wrong.

Crash and Burn

starving
thirsting

amazing
how fast an emotional crash
can happen.

one moment
floating among the clouds

the next
wading through the mire
of sharp, biting syllables

Depression (From the Inside Out)

red
runs through my brain
nerve endings are sensitive

       e v e r y   t h i n g
becomes its own little Broadway drama.

i
shut down.

if i don't
every one
will be caught up in the
hurricane
that consumes my mind.

ocd feeds my depression
the obsessive part of ocd
if i tell you i'm "stalking" you & grin or wink,
i'm mostly joking.

But
there's a part of me that does
                o b s e s s

does wish
to *stalk*

SYNERGY

to get as
                c l o s e
as i can to
you
                (that's why they call it "obsessive")
but that's
illegal and
people would have me committed, so
i
keep a lid on it.

my compulsions aren't usually anything useful, like
cleaning the house.

                No.

i'm compelled to
count
    letters
        numbers
on
        billboards
            license plates and
                various other signage.
                      (boring and very, very useless).

when my obsession(s) is/are,
for whatever reason,
unavailable

to me
either because i'm
attempting
to appear
      normal & sane
or because they're just
      unreachable
for a time
my depression deepens.

                                  (i know...insane.
                                          right?)

the irony:
      i
      don't
      know
if these are
symptoms of
surviving
child sex abuse or
if they'd have been part of my personality
    anyway.

my abuser
took my innocence
                        trauma
rerouted
the synapses in my brain
before my personality could be truly known.

SYNERGY

      i
      don't
      really
      know
who
      i am
who
      i am supposed to be.

Some attempts
at discovery
                          (*writing and editing; motherhood*)
have met with
surprising success.

other attempts
                                    (*marriage*)
have met with
crushing failure.

purple streaks bruise the darkness of my mind
the white-chalk Cliffs of Dover and
long drops
appear suddenly

i weave
                violently
to avoid falling.

sometimes
i fall.

if i'm
lucky
a ledge catches me. if it doesn't,
i fall
into the deep, narrow pit;
     depression.

the sides of the pit are almost completely
 vertical.
    (*where did the hand and toeholds go?*)

some times it takes
    m o n t h s
to emerge
all the while
functioning
attempting to be
    normal
for the sake of those around
me
so they don't wonder and ask

so close to tears
cannot explain what's wrong
not even sure myself
except that

SYNERGY

the demons have come out
    to play
    to taunt
me
with what
i
    don't have
    cannot have
    am not
    never will be.

pushing them back behind the door at the bottom of the pit
    again
securing the padlock that hangs on rusty hinges takes all the
energy
i don't have.

exhausted
i cannot replace
the lock
the rusty hinges
i don't know
    how
        where
to find replacements.

my therapist sees
    the anger
        the desperation

    the depression
    the despair
    the darkness
    that lurk within.
i try not to let others see
what will people think
i don't know if this is
para-menopause or if it's just

Wendy.

is this
depression
ocd, or
symptoms of
something more?

the one constant in my depression is music.
not books
not people
music. instrumental or few lyrics.
this session of depression's playlist
                                    (if you care to know)
has been full of
    enigma's
        a posteriori
        love sensuality devotion
    draconian's
        a rose for the apocalypse

SYNERGY

      turning season within
   really slow motion's
      iron poetry
   chopin's
      nocturnes
   imagine dragons'
      radioactive (from night visions)
   two steps from hell's
      invincible

i don't know how long this bout of
depression
will last.

it started about a week ago.
the last one was
on and off for the whole month of
June
                                  (*as in, 2 months ago*).

it pretty much has to work itself out of my system
    i guess.

i become an automaton
ask no questions
don't want to know
don't really care at this point
struggle to care
can't people

don't adult very well, either
do my work
avoid people as much as possible.

my focus is inward

                                                  selfish.

even my son suffers lack of my attention.
fortunately
he's mostly independent
don't have to worry about being
arrested
for child neglect.

i just can't people
       too much drama
       too many eyes
       too many breaths
  too many hands and fingers and feet and toes
       too many smells
       too many voices
       too much noise

                    JUST
                    TOO
                    MUCH!

i'm a mass of nerve endings
hunch inward around them

SYNERGY

trying to protect them

if you brush up against the wrong one, i might implode
fall apart
(*maybe not in front of you*
that just makes people uncomfortable)
but in private i fall apart
try to keep the implosions to a minimum
because they make the depression worse

there's a lot of
        self-deprecation
        self-flagellation
        self-recrimination
going on inside.

sometimes
i want people to ask questions
just so i know they care
but they usually don't know the
                right
questions to ask
i don't know how to tell them
                which
questions are the right ones
if i knew,

don't you think i'd answer them so i could go back to being me?

ask me what i want
i don't know

i can think of a dozen things
but
will any one of them
      or all of them
pull me
from the depths of this
red, sticky, murky suffering?

i don't know

want to scream
want to beat my head upon the sand
want to box the rock in front of me
      till it's nothing but dust
what will protect my head and fists
      from becoming pulpy masses of torn flesh
      and scarlet rivers of blood

I am
      parched
      starving
      on unfulfilled promises of satiation
      and rainbows at the end of suffering.

SYNERGY

i just want

                            oblivion;

at least

                      temporary insensibility.

. . . maybe tomorrow the sun will shine.

~~effervescent~~ me

I
am not effusive
with emotions,
sentiments.
some
think me unfeeling.

                      on the contrary

I
feel too much.
heart-full reactions
often embarrass;
impede
rational thinking.

if
I
am quiet
in praise
and with thanks
it's because

                      – as goes the cliché –

SYNERGY

still waters run deep
and sometimes
to disturb those depths
is to cause a monsoon.

Freedom (in America)

I'm thankful for freedom (in America).

thankful to live in a country where
    peaceful protest isn't met with government oppression.

(... well ...)

thankful to live in a country where
    leaders are voted out just as easily as they are voted in.

(... so far)

thankful to live in a country where
    I can voice my opinion without fear of reprisal.

(... this is beginning to change)

thankful to live in a country where
    I am free to practice my faith.

(for now)

thankful to live in a country where
    the strong protect the weak.

SYNERGY

(sometimes)

thankful to live in a country where
    anyone can become someone.

(usually)

thankful to live in
    the land of the free and the home of the brave.

(. . . but how long will we be brave and how long will we remain free . . .)

Images of Wilkes-Barre

In my travels
I walk the streets
of a quaint old mining town
that has seen better years.

Architecture at once blighted and beautiful;
buildings sometime stately and proud
give silent witness to bygone attention;
lives long-ago lived, now forsaken.

History lives on, rich and present;
ghosts of a time maybe long forgotten
bright colors weathered and worn.
Walking down the streets, you imagine and sense.

A six-sided star – embedded high in the window
of a house of faith existing
in the midst of the bleakness and gloom –
seems to speak of hope for redemption.

Though barren and worn, some pride remains;
though tired efforts to restore fall short,
still, deserted gables stare with hopeful eyes
peering down at us, following our passage.

SYNERGY

Silent voices screaming in my ears:
"Wait! Come and stay with me.
Gaze out of my windowpane and
keep company with me."

"My inhabitants are all gone away
I've been abandoned for far too long.
Dust coats my casements
my covers are tatters and rags."

The pleading voices fade as we swiftly pass
more pressing matters fill our thoughts;
no time to waste
on ancient and deserted lives.

~~Innocence~~
(to A.B.)

Diamond hard stones of ice
plummet from the sky
blinding shafts of light
shatter the gray
reflects in my eyes, my heart
as I watch you die.

Inspiration

Fingers
fly
over the cool slick keyboard of my
mac.

Muse
speaks
almost quicker than I can
type.

Hurry
must get it all down
before
it fades into the ether of which
dreams
are made.

Journey

A forty-two-foot horseless carriage
   on wheels
sheltering nearly two score
lively
upright characters
   of both sexes.

A collection of independent
   thinkers and doers
Each in their own way
    contributing to the
      humor and chaos of an
        upside-down society.

Everyone of them pursuing
   their own personal
quest
for acceptance and love
   in an immoral society
      often selfish and egotistical.

Free thinkers,
all,
   struggling
     to make

SYNERGY

their mark
upon
  the world
    and fellow humans

Bonding
together
in friendship and trust
  hand in hand they stand –
    poised –
  on the edge of greatness.

Loose Lips Sink Ships

You
word vomit
to
everyone.
I
am blamed because
I
have not yet
learned
    (*even after all these years*) that
you
cannot be
trusted with
anything of
value.

My Future

Standing before the closed door
Sure that it was open
just a moment ago

It's obstructing my path,
no way to get around
Gotta go through or
take another road

So I knock . . . knock,
    beat my fists against the barrier
Shred my fingers,
    bleeding,
to the bone

Can't get past the thought
This is
the only door,
if I can't get through
what will I do...

neglect

Moss grows
white skin
darkened from the sun
no shade
to deflect the blistering rays
and you do nothing.

Whispers caress cheeks
cold fingers reach
for warmth and comfort
questions asked
requests tendered
and you say nothing.

Neglected before
the petals
that tentatively opened
under your shine
draw back inward
to protect the blossom.
And you say nothing.

Off the grid

There's a certain
freedom
in being
untethered
>   (*when your cell service is
>   suspended
>   due to late payments*).

Off the grid

(I have thought about running away
>   many more times
>   as an adult
>   than I ever did
>   as a child.)

Untethered to social media
Who could ever find me
If I didn't want to be found?

Overcast

Today
the sun
hides
behind pewter clouds
while angry winds
whip
verdant palm trees and
the heavens weep.

Tomorrow
cooler, halcyon winds will prevail,
embracing
earth scoured by a monsoon,
caressing
cheeks raised to welcome the returning sunlight,
whispering
playfully through our hair.

Panic Attack

Howl with savage glee
as I bleed

    claws
    talons
    fangs
rend
my flesh.

Heart hammers nails up toward my throat

Too much adrenaline for this
    defective muscle
to handle

Air becomes an even more
precious
commodity than usual. My lungs
wheeze
for breath as I try not to
hyperventilate.

Hands tremble as if I
inherited my long-deceased grandfather's
Parkinson's disease.

SYNERGY

Death grip
bleached-bone white
on my nerves' sanity.

Breakfast churns in my stomach as it
contemplates
a violent exit northward.

A quick dip over the edge into
> *i don't care!*
> *i don't care!*
> *run away!*
> *run away!*

leave it all behind
it doesn't matter
no one cares.

i
    am
        turned
            inside
                out

the death once felt inside
now visible in my flesh.

Do you see
the rents in my canvas
the gaping holes

where my heart and lungs
once resided?

Drawing breath
becomes another battle

I don't know if I can win...

Rainstorm during a traffic jam

A pewter
caul
encircles, domes
the wheeled metal carcasses
moving
at an
     a g o n i z i n g
crawl
across
the massive concrete structure
that shivers
beneath
their collective weight.

hot
sharp
tears
from above
     bombard
the alien forms
in anger, fear, uncertainty.

eyes glowing
     red
          hot heat

SYNERGY

pierce
the heavy veil
descending
without end.

red light

sitting at the red light
i close my eyes
sink into my subconscious
slough off the worries of the day
block out the glare of tail lights
from the vehicle in front of me

feel the light change
from red to green and
wake to the world again.

Silence

It's quiet in here
    silent
    peaceful

Not out there
where I hear
    voices
    music

But here, in this
    headspace
there is nothing.

just

                    Silence

Stronger Than You Think

Do you see the rift in my seams
   the creases in my silk?
Do you see the broken pieces
   of me lying at your feet?

Essence shattered
   soul of me scattered

but I'm stronger than you think.

Dealt a wrenching blow to the core of me
   womb recoils, shrinks inside
the life within, dreams conceived
   miscarried, scar the secret places.

Life in tatters
   each breath bittersweet

but I'm stronger than you think.

Dreams battered, unconscious
   stifled with a blow
lie in secret, smolder
   await the kiss of life.

SYNERGY

Sleep in silence
   a cocoon of safety.

Stronger than you think.

The Summer of His Discontent

Poor little boy
left alone
with friends who care
friends who share
and he's distressed.

Poor little boy
~~survivor~~ victim of neglect
villain of his own story
paints himself black
as the devil.

Poor little boy
refuses
    help
    comfort
    support
from peers or professionals
he's a self-sufficient island
in shark-infested waters.

Needs
    no one
wants
    nothing
but to be left alone.

SYNERGY

Poor little boy
everyone is out to get him
The only word he can scream
is NO!
      over and over
any time his walls are
    breached.

Friends leave one by one
invited to never again share
their own experiences in solidarity.
And he –
     once again
– fills the holes
shores up the weaknesses
in his
walls.

Poor little boy
knows
   all
knows
     nothing
an island of sensitive nerve endings
one touch
sparks the conflagrant fires of self-defense.

Weather Witch (Dennah)

Ribbons of rain
reflect the spirit within
beauty in rage and sorrow
cleansing away impurities

Lighting streaks across the sky
mirrored in my eyes
thunder roars not far away
echoing the inner chaos

Arms raised to the heavens
tears dance with the rain
power owned and accepted

I never wanted this

SOUL

Merriam-Webster: *"the immaterial essence, animating principle, or actuating cause of an individual life; the spiritual principle embodied in human beings..."*

"For what profit is it to a man if he gains the whole world, and loses his own soul? Or what will a man give in exchange for his soul?" **(Matthew 16:26, NKJV)**

A Lifetime Supply
(A reply to "Three Dollars' Worth of God")

I'd like a lifetime supply of Jesus, please
nothing less will appease
    my spirit.
I want more than just three dollars' worth
  so much more than just a brand new birth.

I'd like a lifetime supply of Jesus, please
enough to give me everlasting peace
  enough to set my spirit forever free
    from the sin that had a firm hold on me
enough to set my soul on fire
  with godly courage and spiritual desire.

I want much more than others do, you see
  enough for a lifetime yearning after God
enough to send my soul to heaven eternally
  enough for a lifetime of faith in God
to share that faith with everyone I meet
enough to see me through those pearly gates.

I'd like a lifetime supply of Jesus, please
because nothing less will set me free.

A Prayer for the Dying

how fragile we are
our mortal flesh
clinging to life
by just a thread
    a breath
    a heartbeat

                                               the tip of a fingernail

when it breaks
we're either
thrust into flame
or into serenity
our souls
finding either
unending torment
or eternal peace

A Still Small Voice: Elijah's Song
(I Kings 18 & 19)

The Lord God's victory was great that day.
I was privileged to have a front row seat.
His triumph over the prophets of Baal
at Mount Carmel was complete.
And after three years of famine,
He opened the heavens and the rain fell in sheets.

But then, I'm embarrassed to admit,
a threat from the queen caused me to lose my grit.

*(By the word of the Lord, there was no rain in the land
for three years. Because of the sins of King Ahab,
and his fathers before him, Israel became a wasteland.*

*In the third year, the prophet Elijah called
    for a gathering at Mount Carmel;
    the prophets of Baal against the Lord God of Israel.
It was time for the people to come out from under Baal's
    spell.*

*His priests built an altar. They danced and yelled.
But Baal must have been sleeping or on a journey.
Not even their blood earned his attention;*

SYNERGY

he answered his priests not a word;
no fire fell upon their sacrifice.

Elijah let them exhaust themselves; then
  it was time for God's intervention.)

I built an altar upon twelve stones; one for each Tribe
and called for water to soak the sacrifice,
ignoring the resulting jeers and diatribe.
Then I called to the Lord God of hosts to send fire
and show Israel – once again – that He alone is God.

The flame of the Lord fell from heaven,
  consumed the sacrifice and altar.
All the people fell to their faces and worshiped
  their creator:
The Lord, he is God! The Lord, he is God!
There is no god beside him or greater!

We slew the prophets of Baal, those men of lies and sin
at the brook of Kishon we put them to the sword;
all four hundred and fifty false prophets;
a second sacrifice to the Lord.

I told the king there would be rain
and I went back up the mountain to pray.
I sent my servant to look toward the sea for a sign of rain.
He lacked the faith to see; time and again,

I told him to search the sky for gray.
The seventh time – God's perfect number – he returned
and reported a cloud the size of a man's hand.

I sent him to warn the king: prepare your
    chariot, the rain will not wait for you.
The heavens turned black with clouds, the
    wind roared and there came the rain.
I ran to the city, across the mount and plain.
The Lord gave wings to my feet and I
    arrived before the king in his chariot.

But it was not enough for the king that God sent the rain
he gave a report of all that took place that day to Jezebel,
his queen.
She sent a message to me, venting her spleen,
swearing that she would put me to the sword
    by this time tomorrow.
I will admit: that woman scares me.

So, forgetting all of the wondrous works of the Lord,
    in my fear and despair
I was sure in that moment that God had forsaken me
    and did not care.
I ran to the wilderness a few day's journey from there.
I sat beneath a tree, wallowing in loneliness and self-pity
hoping to find an escape from the things that haunted me.

SYNERGY

Praying that the Lord would take my life himself,
rather than let me perish by the hand of a heathen queen.

I cried aloud to the Lord, my God
and wept bitterly o'er the chastisement of His loving rod
"Why do you not answer me?"
I demanded of the One and Only Deity.
I poured out my troubles and fears to my Master
told Him of the coming disaster.
Then I sat to wait the answer I was sure would come in time
wondering how he would choose to speak this time.

An angel woke me, commanded me to eat.
I did as he bade, then slept again; still
    waiting for an answer.
The angel woke me yet again, commanded me
    to eat in preparation for my journey.
But where was I to go?
Just walk, was the angel's reply.

For forty days and nights I journeyed. The
    Lord brought me to Horeb, the mount of God.
I entered a cave there and waited.

The word of the Lord came and asked, why
    are you here, Elijah?
You sent me here, Lord, I answered. But I
    knew he wanted more,

so I added, I have been jealous for You, Lord;
your children have forsaken You, Your covenant.
They have torn down the altars and put
    Your prophets to the sword.
I alone, am left. They seek to take my life also.

He commanded me to stand upon the mountain.
I did so and awaited the Lord's answer.
The wind began to blow strong and fierce in that place.
And I thought,
    Yes, His mighty hand in the air He will show.
But though I felt the power and might of the wind
His loving hand I could not find.

Still I waited for the answer He had promised to send.
There was a sudden trembling in the ground beneath me
and there appeared a widening rend.
Perhaps my Master had become angry at last and bid the
earth to swallow me.
But the ground stilled and I breathed relief that this time it
was not to be.

After the quaking and rending of the earth
there appeared a mighty fire, roaring for all its worth.
But now I saw that the enemy sought to deceive me
and make me believe in my sight instead of the power I
    cannot see.

SYNERGY

Finally, I felt a rush of warmth, a caress of breath
I lifted up my face in welcome, for I knew this was not
 death.
Instead, to comfort and still my doubts and fears,
this, my Master's choice
the most wondrous peace of all: a still small voice.

I hid my face away from God in shame.
Again He asked, why are you here, Elijah?
Again I said, I have been jealous for You, Lord; Your
children have forsaken Your covenant,
thrown down Your altars and slain Your prophets.
I am the only one left and this heathen queen and her
followers seek to take my life as well.

The Lord chastised me.
I have thousands in all of Israel who have not bowed
unto Baal and his queen.
And I am not finished with you yet, Elijah.
Get you down from this mount and fear not the queen.
In my time, through you and my anointed,
I will make all things right.

Are you happier now?

You left home

too many rules

want to have it
your way
freedom to be, do
what *you* want
no one gainsaying *you*.

Happy now
on your own?

Do you ever
miss
the arms
that love you still
the shoulders
always there for leaning
the smiles
happy just to see you
the peace
you had?

SYNERGY

Is your vision
clearer now?

Is your hearing
sharper now?

Is your future
surer now?

As you were

If he fell in love with you
                as you were
why do you change?

If your beliefs were thus and so
        and he fell in love with you
why do you stop believing?

If your standards were thus and so
        and he fell in love with you
why do your standards change?

If you friends were among this group instead of that
        and he fell in love with you
why do you replace this group of friends with that?

Why do the places you visit
        change?

Why do the friends you keep
        change?

Why do the clothes you wear – the lengths of your skirts
        change?

SYNERGY

Why does the length and color of your hair
    change?

Why do the words you speak
    change?

Why does the look in your eyes
    change?

Why does your beautiful smile
    change?

    (*HE is the common denominator*)

Were you hiding your true self
    before?

Were you pretending to be someone else
    before?

Were you giving lip service to friends and loved ones

    and God

  before?

Were you crying out for help
      before?

Do you feel freer
      now?

Do you love yourself more
      now?

Are you happier
      now?

Does he love you
      MORE
      now?

Do you have more control
      now?

Or is the new – sadder – you
      the one crying out for help
now?

If he was
just
an excuse

SYNERGY

To finally do something that had been
        in your heart
        on your mind
        urging you
anyway,
Then I get it;
    I do.

I was there,
        many moons ago.
And discovered

                              (*as I hope you do not*)

That the one for whom I
            changed
        wasn't *worth* my time
        wasn't *worth* my effort
        wasn't *worth* my shame

Least of all, a change of
        who I had been
        into something

                Less.

Candle-less

Promise of
peace is
forgotten in
cares of today.

The
rope that swings from
heaven
offering an
escape
from madness,
hangs
in shadow.

Where is the
candle
to illuminate the night?

Does God Make Mistakes?

Does God make mistakes?

Male *and* **Female** created He

                         them.

             (Male = He/Him
             Female = She/Her)

Gender
    doesn't
        change

yesterday
you were born a girl

today
you *feel* like you're a boy

                 instead.

             How
             do
             you
             know?

SYNERGY

How do you

                  know

what it
    feels like
    looks like
    is like
                  to be a boy?

I am a mother

but some days I wake up
not wanting to be
a mother.

So I should just

                  a b a n d o n

my child
    my responsibilities
    my joys
    my heartaches
    my triumphs

as

                  a mother?

and become...

what?

By the act of giving birth,
no matter how I
> feel
> think
> act

I will

ALWAYS
BE
A
MOTHER

I may assume the
role
of "father"
but I will

NEVER

be
> a
>> *father*.

God is perfect. His creation is perfect.

SYNERGY

Humans are fallible

we

make mistakes all the time.

How do you know that

you

aren't the one making the mistake?

Forget Me Not

When the road you are led to travel
seems riddled with pits and always uphill
when you try so hard and all you gain is ill
Forget Me not.

When your struggle for survival seems utterly in vain
and all around the enemy waits for your fall
when you wonder who'll answer when you call,
Forget Me not.

I Am the One who created you
    Trust Me
    lean upon Me
    walk in My Way
    follow the map of My Word
I'll feed your soul.
Forget Me not.

You'll find an easier path
filled with joy and peace, not matter the trial
turn to Me in sorrow and in joy, I'll help you win this race.
Forget Me not.

Formed in the Fire

The shapeless metal
    screams
in anguish
as it is thrust into the fire
questioning
why its master puts it through
so much torment
so much pain

The steel softens,
becomes red hot.

Just as it grows used to the heat,
it is taken from the fire
only to be
  held
    down
      upon the anvil

Sudden fear becomes reality
as the unyielding hammer
    beats
      mercilessly
upon the blade

SYNERGY

      driving
all imperfections from its surface

again
      the agony
again
      the screams of torment

The longing
for death
to come and end its suffering.

But the metal does not see
                the tears
its Maker weeps in empathy
despite the determination to
succeed.

Grace (or, The Golden Trumpet Tree)

I parked 'neath
the golden trumpet tree
that grows in my parents' yard.

Rains fell and winds gusted
flowers plummeted
from the tree
like tears.

On the wet, fertile grass
or hard, sterile concrete
they landed;

all but one.

It rested on my windshield
abiding the quick, fierce ballyhoo,
its brilliant petals dimmed and drenched.

It greeted me, as I prepared to drive away,
its yellowness
reviving
in the warmth
of the sun that had broken through
storm clouds

SYNERGY

to shine a ray on the
single golden trumpet
that the tree gifted
to me.

He Came

He came
He came
we were unworthy
but
                         still
He came.

He bled
He bled and died
we were unworthy
but
                         still
He bled and died
for us.

We mocked
we mocked
but
                         still
He loved us.

He came,
an innocent babe
vulnerable and frail and human as we

SYNERGY

yet
the Son of God was He.

Perfect, this child
born of a virgin
his first bed, a manger of hay.
angels, the messengers of his birth.

An existence of
    toil
    trial
    temptation
    sorrow
    ingratitude.

                         still

humble he became
to better relate to us
His greatest creation. And
    we
        mocked
             Him
    we
        flogged
             Him
    we
        crucified

> Him.

And yet…

And yet…

STILL

His love for us grows ever stronger
    no matter our denial
Never has He forsaken us
    no matter our rebellion
Never has He given up on us
    no matter our failings.

He is still

always loving
never failing
    Creator
    Father
    Savior
    King.

One day
One day

SYNERGY

He will return
the heavens will part
He will split the skies
we will rise to meet him in the air
He will carry us
Home.

He came.
He came.

And

He is coming back

again.

Hope Renewed

Broken heart
  broken soul
    broken spirit
      broken mind
        broken life: all torn apart...

Shattered dreams
  shattered faith
    shattered hopes
      shattered trust
        shattered life: falling apart at the seams...

Worship through it all
  worship through the brokenness
    worship through the shattered bits
      worship through the tears
        worship when you fall...

Praise though you feel torn
  praise though you feel broken
    praise though you feel shattered
      praise though you're falling apart
        praise though you're tired and worn...

SYNERGY

He is near those that are of a broken heart
  He will never leave you, nor forsake you
    His strength is made perfect in your weakness
      He will not put upon you more than you can bear
      He heals the wounds of the broken-hearted.

Not My Will

Struggle, tug of war
   stubborn rebellious will
I sink into the mire
   down, descending further still.

Struggling for survival
   always trying my own way
looking to my own path
   ignoring the road before me.

Staggering 'neath a heavy load
   trying to bear it on my own
afraid to ask for aid
   bowed down with my own desires.

Struck by what I cannot add
   to my already tiresome burden
I sink to my knees, raise weary eyes;

            "Not my will."

Our Weakness; His Strength

Sometimes our trials overwhelm us
struggles seem far beyond our strength to bear
confused, overburdened, we falter, stumble, fall
wondering where we went wrong.

His strength is made perfect
in our weakness
God promised to be near us
through all our days – bad or good;
He'll never leave us alone.

We are in a battle we cannot win alone
He gives us armor, a shield and sword.
take up your defenses, even through your trials
just stand;
He'll be right beside you.

When you don't feel Him near
when you can't see His hand
remember His promises
and just stand.

His strength is made perfect
in our weakness

SYNERGY

He gives us grace to bear our trials
        no more than we can stand
and
even when we feel all alone
He is right there, holding our hand.

Recovery

Gather the tattered fragments of abused emotions around
    me
        a garment old, worn and frayed.
Muster the remains of dignity cast aside, to me
        attempt to regain self-esteem, for which I dearly paid.

Pick up my heart, scrub off the smut
        that's caked it far too long
set my soul back on the straight path; out of the rut
        I wallowed in, even knowing it was wrong.

Look to God for strength and peace each day
        hope and pray He'll not fail me, too.
Ask for help and temperance along the way;
        trust He'll be beside me in all I do.

Some Sound Advice

Forget...don't think...don't hurt
   Pray without ceasing.

Ease your mind...converse without words
   Study to be quiet.

Don't dwell on thoughtlessness of others
   Do unto others as you would have them do to you.

Think carefully before you speak...don't speak in anger
   Be angry and sin not.

Do not despair...do not loose heart
   Trust in the Lord with all thine heart.

Don't go your own way...don't fall from the path
   There is a way that seems right...the end thereof is death.

Splinter

I am conceived in your mind and heart –
perhaps someone said something you did not like
or your soul was not sincere from the start
and you were only looking for a fight.
Anyway, you know I'm there, and still you let me stay
after all, I'm just a little thing...

Eventually, I will keep you out of church
in your mind, daily perch.
I will fester in your soul
a smoldering little piece of coal.
I will keep you away from God...
but I'm just a little thing...

I will draw you away from your friends
and lead you down countless dead ends.
You will find new people to be with
they will help your soul continue to wither.
I will make you ignore everything
but, I'm just a little thing...

I will tear you away from blessings to come
towards God your mind will numb
I will reduce you to nothing
stealing everything you've worked for

SYNERGY

still, you will not lance the sore
after all, I'm just a little thing...

You will lose feeling for those you love
while deep inside wishing you'd fled me
when I was just a seed within your mind.

I will destroy you when I mature
you'd better root me out while clearly you still can see
for I will not always be just a little thing.

Stumble or Rise

Adversity comes
      will you stumble and fall
      or step and climb to the top?

Crisis hits
      will you rise
      or face your demise?

Trauma happens
      will you be a victor
      or a victim?

Trouble comes to all
what separates
the victor
from
the victim
is progression or regression.

will it make you
or
will it break you?

Surrender

Empty and unhappy, searching for something to fill the void inside
travel the first crooked path you find
stopping every few miles to taste the wares along the wayside
believing in a lie that's soothing to your mind.

Trusting in things temporal
led astray down a dark road, unwilling to see the Light
while deep inside, your soul cries for something lasting and eternal
knowing you'll not find it wandering in the night.

Only Jesus can satisfy
only He can fill the soul-void.
Surrender to the Creator
His Spirit will fill you, make you new and whole.

That Sounds Like Home to Me

There is a wonderful place
filled with beauty and with grace
    someday this wondrous place I'll see;
    that sounds like home to me.

Walls of jasper, streets of gold
in that place we'll never grow old
    forever with my Lord I'll be;
    that sounds like home to me.

Soon my cares and toils will be gone at last
the loneliness of this life will all be past
    my blessed Savior's face I'll see;
    that sounds like home to me.

I'll meet again
family and friends
who've gone on before;
that sounds like home to me.

Some glorious day
I'll be on my way
    that heavenly place above I'll see;
    that sounds like home to me.

SYNERGY

A beautiful song I'll sing
the praises of my Lord to ring
    finally that heavenly place I'll see;
    oh, that sounds like home to me!

What does God do?

What does God do
when people
forget Him
begin to act like
He is either not there
or He doesn't care?

What does God do
when we leave Him out
of our busy lives
when we begin denying
His omniscience and omnipresence?

Does God ever wish
He'd never given us
free will?

Does He ever get sick and tired of us turning our backs to Him,
denying Him?
     He who created us

People talk about God's wrath and then
wonder how could "He allow" bad things to happen to
"good" people.

SYNERGY

What makes us "good" people?

and what makes "good" people any less deserving of "bad" things than those who are not considered "good" people?

Why do we blame
God
when we
                – human beings –
are responsible for our own grief and torment?

Why is it
God's fault
when it's
                cause and effect:
                humans exercising
                    free will

Which Path?

Which path will be your choice?
the Way that is narrow
or
the way that is broad?

The narrow straight path
that leads to Life
or
the broad winding path
that leads to death?

The Rock that is firm and stable
or
the sand that shifts beneath your feet?

There will be storms
even upon the Rock
there will be battles and scars
      but
      you
      will
      stand.

There will be storms
upon the sand

SYNERGY

the powdery grains will
shift beneath you
      and
      you
      will
      fall.

Publishing Acknowledgements

pretty little girl – Feminine Collective
(http://www.femininecollective.com/pretty-little-girl-trigger-warning/)

~~effervescent~~ me – Feminine Collective
(http://www.femininecollective.com/effervescent-me/)

love. (lost?) – Feminine Collective
(http://www.femininecollective.com/love-lost/) (also published in FC's *Love Notes From Humanity*)

game of hearts – C. Streetlights (http://cstreetlights.com/game-hearts/)

About the Author

Wendy C. Garfinkle is a South Florida-based writer, freelance editor and manuscript designer, and the publisher of Emery Press Books. Her editing repertoire includes newspapers (both collegiate and daily), court transcripts and depositions, nonprofit grants, technical manuals, essays, blogs, a religious newsletter, and manuscripts for multiple Indie publishers.

She holds (among others), MA and MFA degrees in Creative Writing from Wilkes University in Pennsylvania.

Wendy is an avid reader and traveler who loves caffeine, storms, and dark chocolate. In addition to freelance, Wendy works in law enforcement, and is involved in ministry at her church.

www.ingramcontent.com/pod-product-compliance
Lightning Source LLC
Chambersburg PA
CBHW050355120526
44590CB00015B/1707